EXECUTIVE EDITORS
Sarah Galbraith, Alan Doan,
Jenny Doan, David Mifsud

MANAGING EDITOR
Natalie Earnheart

CREATIVE DIRECTOR
Christine Ricks

PHOTOGRAPHER
BPD Studios

CONTRIBUTING PHOTOGRAPHER
Katie Whitt

VIDEOGRAPHER
Jake Doan

DESIGNER & TECHNICAL WRITER
Linda Johnson

PROJECT DESIGN TEAM
Natalie Earnheart, Jenny Doan,
Sarah Galbraith

AUTHOR OF PATCHWORK MURDER
Steve Westover

CONTRIBUTING COPY WRITERS
Katie Mifsud, Jenny Doan, Camille Maddox,
Natalie Earnheart, Christine Ricks, Alan
Doan, Sarah Galbraith

COPY EDITOR
Geoff Openshaw

CONTRIBUTING PIECERS
Jenny Doan, Natalie Earnheart,
Stephen Nixdorf, Cassie Nixdorf

CONTRIBUTING QUILTERS
Bernice Kelly, Deloris Burnett, Jamey Stone,
Betty Bates, Emma Jensen, Sherry Melton,
Cassie Martin, Amber Weeks, Sandi Gaunce,
Daniela Kirk, Amy Gertz, Patty St. John, Mari
Zullig, Megan Gilliam, Lauren Dorton, Sam
Earnheart

CONTACT US
Missouri Star Quilt Co
114 N Davis
Hamilton, Mo. 64644
888-571-1122
info@missouriquiltco.com

content

HELLO
from MSQC

When my kids were young enough to enjoy a summer break from school, August always seemed to come too quickly. Once it arrived, a panicky feeling reminded us that the fun of summer was coming to an end too soon. We loved those last days of summer, and we crammed in as much fun as we could. Vacations, trips to the beach, hiking in the mountains, camping, and picnics—goodness those were the days! But above all else, I especially loved road trips.

Everyone had their own pillow and quilt in the car, and once on the road, those quilts became barriers, beds, and tents. I had these great "pockets" that attached to the back of the car seats. They were full of everything I could possibly dream up to keep kids busy: pencils, paper, small toys, and snacks. My kids loved them!

Going on trips with that many children wasn't easy, but when I was a young mom, I heard a story that I have never forgotten. A man told me that every year he saved money to redo his bathroom and every year he ended up spending that money going on a vacation. He said he couldn't imagine the kids calling home and saying, "Remember the time we remodeled the bathroom?" So with that in mind, off we went on our crazy road trips, laughing, fighting, loving, and singing—and all at the top of our lungs.

My husband and I have now passed the baton to the next generation, but I still provide the quilts (and sometimes a few cookies) to those traveling families. Even if you're not the one cleaning up the spilled juice box, breaking up a sibling war, or singing "John Jacob Jingleheimer Schmidt," in a way you are still going along for the adventure, creating lifelong memories as the long, free days of summer draw to a close.

We hope that as you prepare for the shift in seasons that you and your loved ones are able to enjoy the memories of long summer days while looking forward to a resplendent and cozy fall.

" We hope our magazine— BLOCK will inspire you to create beautiful quilts. "

Jenny

JENNY DOAN
MISSOURI STAR QUILT CO

4

cooler evenings

In the summer evenings as a kid I would often take my bike and ride to this special-to-me spot and watch the sun set. Watching the summer sky change always amazed me. How did it manage to go from bright azure blues, to sunny yellows and fire-in-the-sky reds and pinks in a matter of minutes? I knew if I closed my eyes I'd miss it. I'd sit waiting until the last peek of light could be seen and the crickets would begin to chirp their evening song. It was magical—a place for me to explore my hopes and dreams.

These days I don't have as much time to stop and enjoy the setting sun. But when I do find a minute, it still stuns me how wonderful and different each sunset can be.

The palette of colors inspires me just as much as those sunsets of my childhood. I still love to find a secluded spot to be alone with my thoughts just like I did years ago. It helps to rejuvenate my soul and open up my creativity.

So, go enjoy a sunset—or savor this fun-inspired palette of color. Let it remind you that creativity can be found anywhere and be influenced by anything!

CHRISTINE RICKS
MSQC Creative Director, BLOCK MAGAZINE

SOLIDS

FBY13018 RJR Fabric - Tropicana
SKU-9617-339

FBY13017 RJR Fabric - Flamingo
SKU-9617-338

FBY12994 RJR Fabric - Blue Bayou
SKU-9617-300

FBY12972 RJR Fabric - Riviera
SKU-9617-274

FBY12989 RJR Fabric - Cove
SKU-9617-294

FBY8514 RJR Fabric - Tormaline
SKU- 9617-103

PRINTS

FBY14383 Wee Wander - Summer Ride Melon
by Sarah Jane for Michael Miller Fabrics
SKU-DC6227-MELO-D

FBY14107 Up Parasol - Devon Check
by Heather Bailey for Free Spirit Fabrics
SKU-PWHB045.PERSI

FBY14752 Christmas Pure & Simple -
Starry Dots Cobalt
by Nancy Halvorsen for Benartex Fabrics
SKU-0438555B

FBY15005 Trail Mix - Picnic teal
by Bo Bunny for Riley Blake
SKU-C4016-TEAL

FBY14374 Wee Wander - Nature Walk Turquoise
by Sarah Jane for Michael Miller Fabrics
SKU-DC6229-TURQ-D

FBY11966 Garden Party Tango-Medallion
by Melissa Ybarra of Iza pearl Design
for Windham Fabrics
SKU-388896-6

Slice of *life*

quilt designed by JENNY DOAN

When I was a kid we had a tree house in our backyard. I could spend hours up in it playing with friends or even all by myself. So when I had my own kids, I made sure we had a tree house of our own in our backyard. It was a great way to spend some quality time as a family. I still treasure those memories of easy afternoons spent out in the sunshine together. Something is so sentimental about the simplicity of childhood days, when a game of red rover or looking for lost pirate ships could fill your day with happiness.

I was amazed at how easy it was to add a little magic to my young children's lives—pancakes made in the shape of their initials, wintertime picnics in the living room, or one-on-one trips to get forty-nine cent ice cream cones. It didn't have to take a lot of effort or money to make them feel special and loved.

> " I still treasure those memories of easy afternoons spent out in the sunshine together. "

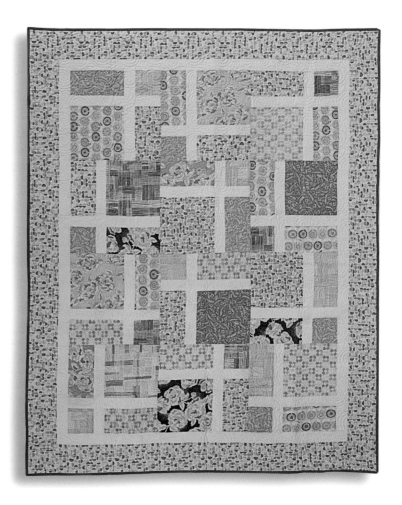

When we first made this quilt and decided to call it Slice of Life it immediately brought to mind all the sack lunches I made for the kids when they were school age. It didn't take much to add a little fun to these lunches.

There was always a sandwich involved, of course. Sometimes I cut the sandwich diagonally, into two triangles. Sometimes I cut into four squares. Sometimes I even used a cookie cutter to give the sandwich a fun shape. But the cutest trick I ever used was to write messages on the bread with lemon juice. By toasting the bread, the message would magically appear!

Even on days that I didn't have time to write secret lemon juice messages, I still made sure the children got a note of

some sort in their lunch. I just wanted to brighten their day and let them know how much I loved them.

Those simple little gestures really do mean so much. In fact, when my husband and I celebrated our thirty-year anniversary, Jacob made a video of all the kids sharing memories and one of the topics that came up was my sack lunches.

What a thrill to realize that after all these years my kids still remember the little, everyday things we did to make their childhood sweeter. There is no better feeling than knowing you have made a difference in the life of a child. Other achievements pale in comparison to the memories of special times shared with family.

materials

makes a 64" X 80" layer cake quilt

QUILT TOP
- 1 layer cake
- ½ jelly roll **OR** 1½ yds solid fabric
- 1¼ yds outer border

BINDING
- ½ yd coordinating fabric

BACKING
- 5 yds 44" wide **OR** 2 yds 90" wide

SAMPLE QUILT
- **Palermo** by Erin Mcmorris for Westminster
- **Bella Solids White (98)** by Moda Fabrics

1 basic block

To create the basic quilt block, first make a giant 9-patch using layer cakes and adding sashing.

From sashing fabric cut (4) 2½" strips (or use JR strips); subcut into:

> (6) 10" strips &
> (2) 33" strips

Lay out 9 squares in an eye-pleasing 3 x 3 configuration. Sew (2) 10" sashing strips between the layer cake squares as you sew each row together. Press to the sashing. Next, add (2) 33" sashing strips between the 3 rows as you sew them together.

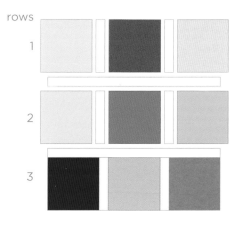

1 make a giant 9-patch with sashing

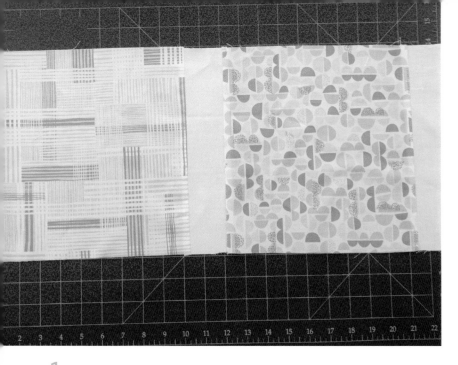

1 Build (3) rows of 3 layer cakes with sashing between the squares.

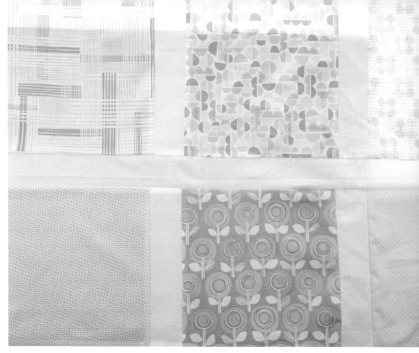

2 Add (2) sashing strips between the rows. Press to the sashing.

3 Once the layer cake 9-patch is fully assembled, cut it in half down the middle vertically and horizontally. Measure 4¾" from the sashing.

2 cut

Cut the 9-patch once down the center vertically; once through the center horizontally. Folding the 9-patch in half and ironing a crease will help create a cutting guide line. Or, you can cut 4¾" from the sashing. Repeat steps 1 & 2 an additional 2 more times.

Yield: (12) 16½" blocks

3 arrange & sew

Arrange the entire quilt center into a 3 x 4 grid turning the blocks so that seams do not intersect.

Sew blocks together by rows, pressing seams in one direction for even rows; in the opposite directions for odd rows.

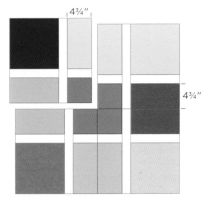

2 cut each 9-patch into 4 equal blocks

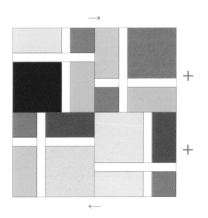

3 arrange the blocks so that seams do not intersect

HIDDEN BENEFIT: *There are no points to match in this quilt. Yippee!*

Sew the rows together nesting seams as you go. Press.

Quilt Center Size: 48½" x 64½"

4 borders

Use (7) 2½" strips for the inner border. Follow steps in *construction basics* to attach to the quilt. **A-D** Press to the borders.

Cut (7) 6" strips of outer border fabric.

Attach to the quilt in the same manner as the inner border.

5 quilt & bind

Layer quilt top on batting and backing and quilt the way you like. Square up all raw edges.

Cut (8) 2½" strips from binding fabric to finish. See *construction basics* for greater detail.

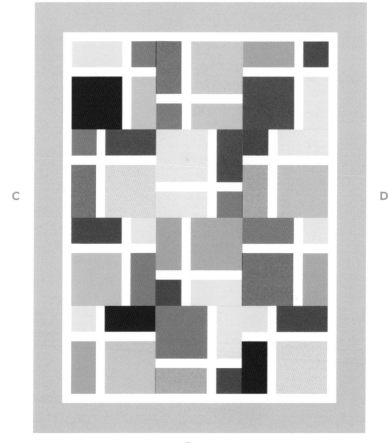

4 add borders in the order **A-D**; always measure the quilt top before cutting the borders

Disappearing hourglass

quilt designed by JENNY DOAN

A while back I was teaching a group in Idaho how to make the Disappearing Pinwheel Block. A sweet gal named Glenna brought her pieces up to me in a stack and said, "I don't know what I have done, but I just can't make this work!"

I laid out the pieces to put the blocks together and quickly discovered the problem: she had sewn her block together as an hourglass rather than a pinwheel. But all was not lost! As we played around with the block, we discovered several new patterns each as fun and interesting as the intended disappearing pinwheel. And thus the disappearing hourglass block was born! It hadn't been planned, but it certainly was a happy accident!

Happy accidents are all around us, making life sweeter than we could have ever planned. I have a friend named Afton who, after staying home to raise her children to school-age, had settled comfortably into her career as a nurse in a newborn nursery. Life, it seemed, had gone according to plan and Afton felt content and fulfilled in her new duties.

Nothing could have surprised her more than when, at the age of forty, Afton discovered that she was once again pregnant! She worried about the demands of caring for a baby while juggling five older children and a full time job. She worried that she was too old and too busy to keep up with the energy and needs of a new tiny person. And deep down, she mourned the impending loss of this comfortable stage of life, the rhythm and predictability the family had developed over the years. But all doubts and disappointment were quickly washed away when her precious new daughter arrived, tiny and pink.

They named the baby girl Joy, and she certainly lived up to her name. Joy was a radiantly happy girl with bouncing ringlets and sparkling blue eyes. She seemed to carry sunshine with her everywhere she went. Looking back, Afton often remarked that the arrival of Joy marked the beginning of the happiest time of her life. "Everyone should have a baby at forty!" she would say.

When life gives you lemons, make lemonade, of course! But don't forget to take a moment to realize that lemonade may have been exactly what you wanted all along, so thank goodness those lemons showed up! Unplanned and unwanted are two very different things. So embrace all those happy accidents you meet along the way. Call it serendipity, call it dumb luck, call it divinity: life just wouldn't be as rich if everything went according to plan!

materials

makes a 72¼" X 83½" layer cake quilt

QUILT TOP
- 1 print layer cake
- 1 solid layer cake OR 2½ yds solid
- ½ yd inner border
- 1¼ yd outer border

BINDING
- ½ yd coordinating fabric

BACKING
- 5 yds or 2¼ yds 90"

SAMPLE QUILT
- **Miss Kate** by Bonnie & Camille for Moda
- **Bella Solids Snow (11)** by Moda Fabrics

1 sew

Pair two layer cakes RST (right sides together)—one light, one dark. Sew a ¼" seam all around. You can stop and turn a quarter inch before the end or simply sew off the end—your choice.

2 cut

Sometimes this step goes faster with a rotating cutting mat. With your rotary cutter cut across the layer cake diagonally twice—4 half square triangles (HST). Press seams to the darker side. Repeat 30 times.

3 hourglass block

Arrange the 4 HSTs to create an hour-

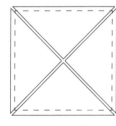

1 pair up RST   2 cut diagonally twice

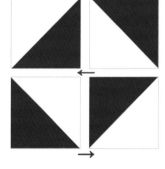

3 build hourglass-in-a-square

1 If you line the ruler up with the center seam you will cut 2⅛″ on both sides of it. Repeat for the horizontal center seam as well.

2 The hourglass will be cut into (9) 4¼″ square sections.

3 Just by turning the 8 outside blocks 180 degrees and the center block 90 degrees a whole new block will appear.

2⅛″   4¼″

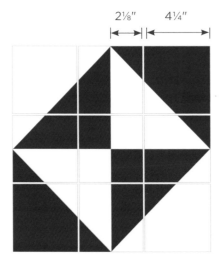

4 cut the hourglass block into 9 sections; 4 cuts

glass-in-a-square. Follow the diagram. Sew HSTs in rows first RST. Press to the dark side. Sew the two rows together nesting the center seam. Make 30

4 cut

Square up the hourglass to 12¾″ symmetrically. This will make cutting in thirds much easier. Each of the 9 squares will measure 4¼.″ This measurement divided by 2 (=2⅛″) will allow you to use the center seams as the cutting guides. Line up the ruler with a center seam. Cut 2⅛″ away from the center seam on both sides, turning the block as needed without disturbing it. This is where a rotating cutting mat comes in handy. Repeat for the other center seam.

5 turn & sew

Turn each of the 8 outside squares 180°—the center 90.° Follow the diagram. Sew the 3 blocks of each row together first. Press according to the arrows. Sew rows together nesting seams. You may want to repress the seams that intersect with the center square in order to nest them.

Block size: 11¾″ x 11¾″
Yield: 30 blocks

6 layout & sew

Lay out the blocks in a 5 x 6 grid in an eye-pleasing fashion. Sew blocks together in rows; then rows together to form the quilt center. Pressing all seams

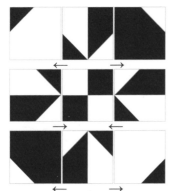

5 turn and sew back together

A

C

D

B

6 match solid to solid, print to print throughout; the small print hourglass surrounded by white will appear as the quilt comes together

to the same side in even rows; to the opposite side in odd rows will help when nesting seams.

Quilt center: 56¾" x 68"

7 borders
From the inner border fabric cut (7) 2½" strips. Follow steps in *construction basics* to attach to the quilt. **A-D** Press to the borders.

Cut (7) 6" strips of outer border fabric. Attach to the quilt in the same manner as the inner border.

8 quilt & bind
Layer quilt top on batting and backing and quilt the way you like. Square up all raw edges.

Cut (8) 2½" strips from binding fabric to finish. See *construction basics* for more detail.

tag *team*

quilt designed by NATALIE EARNHEART

When geese fly in a V formation, the lead goose works the hardest, providing an extra boost of airflow that lifts the birds following behind, allowing them to have an easier ride and rest their wings for a while. But like any of us, that head goose can't keep it up indefinitely, and eventually another goose takes its place in the formation. Each goose takes a turn leading the way and each goose takes a turn coasting. The geese do this continually during long, migratory flights, not short sprints.

Likewise, for us, the long journey of life is easiest when we are able to share our burdens. In marriage, for example, my husband and I realized a long time ago that if one of us is panicked, stressed, or otherwise emotionally out of commission, the other one has to step up and carry the load for both of us. This has happened many times. When I was a young mom with small kids, there were several days when my husband came to the rescue. Once,

" I believe that families and friends are at their best when they mirror that flock of geese flying in a V. Sometimes we have the energy to lead the way and other times we need to lean on others. "

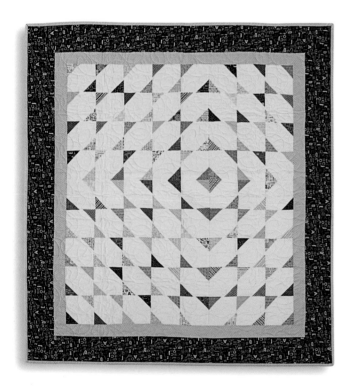

The layout of this quilt is what makes it so special...you take a simple ordinary block and change up the layout and it becomes EXTRAORDINARY!

he walked into the house after work and I just wordlessly handed him the baby with a poopy diaper and left to take a walk while he soothed the crying toddler and cleaned up our burned dinner.

But sometimes the tables have turned and I've needed to step up for my husband. Once, when a close friend of my husband passed away at far too young an age, I made all the flight and hotel arrangements for us to go to the funeral and let him simply mentally check-out. Sometimes you just need to excuse yourself from life for a little while.

I believe that families and friends are at their best when they mirror that flock of geese flying in a V. Sometimes we have the energy to lead the way and other times we need to lean on others. We may not be heading south for the winter, but by admitting that sometimes we need to rely on someone else, we just might get through this journey that we're all on together. This kind of tag-team pattern is essential to keep from burning out.

This is also the reason I love the idea of the flying geese pattern. The quilt is beautiful and the pattern is a constant reminder about the value of leaning on each other as family and friends on our own, long migration of life.

materials

makes a 50" X 55½" charm pack quilt

QUILT TOP
- ½ charm pack print
- 2 charm pack solids
- ½ yd inner border
- ¾ yd outer border

BINDING
- ½ yd coordinating fabric

BACKING
- 3¼ yds

SAMPLE QUILT
- **Elementary** by Sweetwater for Moda Fabrics
- **Bella Solids Snow (11)** by Moda Fabrics

1 cut

Cut (18) *printed* charm squares in fourths. You now have (72) 2½" print squares.

2 fold & press

Fold each 2½" print square in half diagonally and press. This will be your sewing line.

3 snowball

To snowball or employ the "stitch & flip" technique means to add a triangle from a different fabric to corners of blocks. Mix your print squares to achieve a patchwork

 TIP: *the fold should never begin in the corner.*

1 cut (18) 5" charms squares in fourths: (72) 2½" squares

fold line

2 the fold stretches from side to side

28

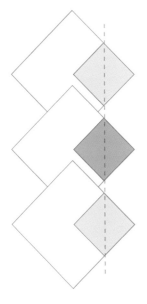

3 chain piecing for quicker assembly

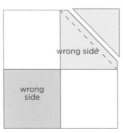

3 snowball & trim the corners

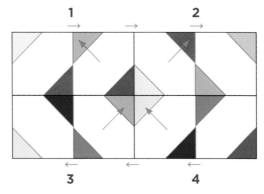

4 There are 2 block orientations: upper corner pointed left (quadrants 1 & 4) & upper corner pointed right (quadrants 2 & 3)

Note: *There are only a few points to match in this whole quilt!*

look. Use a solid 5″ charm square. Lay a print square RST on a corner. The fold should cross the corner diagonally from one side to the other.

Chain piecing will make this step go quickly. It's an assembly line method of sewing fabric together. Feed a square and a rectangle RST through the sewing machine using a ¼″ seam. Continue sewing off the fabric a few stitches and feed the next block

through the machine and so on. Select needle down on your machine for better results. Snip threads to separate blocks. Trim excess fabric to ¼″ and press open. Repeat for the opposite corner.

Block size: 5″ x 5″

4 layout

The quilt is layed out in an 8 x 9 grid composed of 4 quadrants that meet to form the central hourglass. In quadrants 1 & 4 the scrappy corners are facing up to the left; in 2 & 3, up to the right. Following this pattern lay out the entire quilt center adding blocks to each quadrant.

In our example the hourglass forms in the 5th column over and the 4th row down. But feel free to position the hourglass anywhere you want it!

Once you are satisfied with the layout, sew blocks together to make a row. Press all seams in one direction in the first row; in the opposite direction in the second row and so on. Sew rows together nesting seams. Press.

Quilt center: 36½″ x 41″

5 borders

From the inner border fabric cut (5) 2½″ strips. Follow steps in *construction basics* to attach to the quilt. **A-D** Press to the borders.

Cut (5) 5″ strips of outer border fabric. Attach to the quilt in the same manner as the inner border.

6 quilt & bind

Layer quilt top on batting and backing and quilt the way you like. Square up all raw edges.

Cut (6) 2½″ strips from binding fabric to finish. See *construction basics* for greater detail.

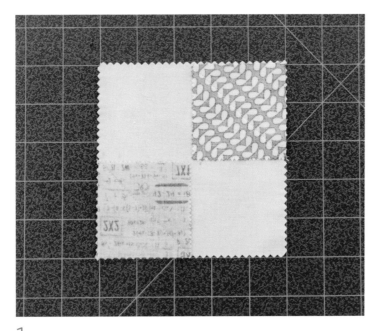

1 Snowball the opposite corners of the solid square

2 Trim to ¼" seam.

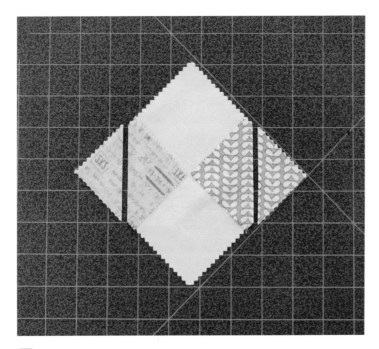

3 Remove excess fabric.

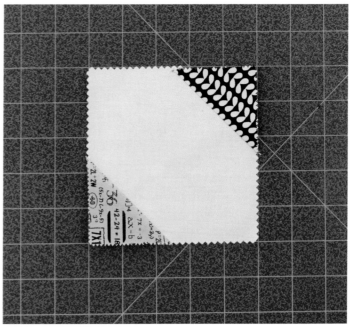

4 Flip open. Press.

A

C

D

B

Lovely Leaves

quilt designed by JENNY DOAN

Fall always comes so suddenly. Summer days seem to stretch, one after another, into one long, hot daydream. Then, one morning, you wake up to a little nip in the air. All of a sudden there is a freshness, a jolt of change. My husband always says, "The air smells like football tonight!" I'm not much of a football fan myself, but those autumn evenings sure do have a chilly snap of excitement to them.

Along with fall come the leaves—lots of leaves. When I was a girl, I loved to rake leaves with my mom. She'd show us how to rake them up into rows to form "houses" with different little rooms. We could play for hours in our imaginary homes made of crispy, golden leaves. A small pile of leaves became a pillow, a plop of 4 or 5 on a frisbee plate became "dinner." Every year I could hardly wait for the leaves to start to change color and fall to the ground.

Now that I'm a grandma, I love to invite my little grandchildren over to play in the leaves. We rake them all into a huge pile on a tarp, and that's when the fun begins. We jump and play and swim through a sea of crunchy yellows and reds.

When the kids aren't looking, my husband quietly buries himself deep in the pile of leaves and waits. "Where did Grandpa go?" I call innocently, then screams and giggles erupt as Grandpa bursts out of his hiding place with a growl and plenty of tickles.

At long last we load the kids onto the tarp with the leaves and give them a ride all the way to a ditch. We dump those leaves (and sometimes a kid or two!) into the ditch and head home for a cup of hot chocolate.

Fall is such an exciting time, but it seems to go as quickly as it comes. Those brilliant autumn colors are often hidden under a blanket of white long before I'm ready to say goodbye. Capturing the fleeting magic of fall in a quilt like the Lovely Leaves Quilt is a great way to be able to enjoy the season all year round and remember the fun we always have during "leaf time."

materials
makes a 58" X 64" jelly roll quilt

QUILT TOP
- 1 jelly roll prints
- 2¼ yds solid
- 1 yd outer border

BINDING
- ½ yd coordinating fabric

BACKING
- 3¾ yds coordinating fabric

SAMPLE QUILT
- **Burlap Solids** by Bernartex
- **Bella Solids White** (98) by Moda Fabrics

1 cut

From each print JR strip cut (14) 2½" squares and (2) 3½" x 1½" strips. Cut carefully. 1 JR strip = 2 blocks. Use (36) JR strips.

From the solid fabric cut:
    (27) 2½" WOF strips;
    subcut into 2½" squares

2 organize

For each block, group together:
    (6) solid squares
    (7) print squares &
    (1) print rectangle

Total: 72 blocks

7x - 2½"   **6x** - 2½"

1x - 3½" x 1½"

2 after cutting, organize the elements for each block

fold & sew line

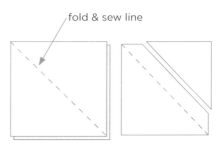

2 pair 1 print & 1 solid RST; sew on fold line; trim ¼"; press; make 4 for each block

1   To make an HST (half square triangle) either press or draw a diagonal line across a 2½" square. Pair with a solid and sew on the line.

2   Trim to ¼" seam allowance. Press to the dark side. Make 4 HSTs for each leaf.

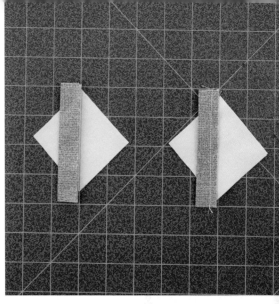

3   Stem block: line the raw edges of a 3½" folded WST rectangle to the center line of a 2½" solid square. Sew ¼" along the raw edges. Press the stem over the raw edges and topstitch down.

4   Trim off excess stem fabric so the block is again 2½" square.

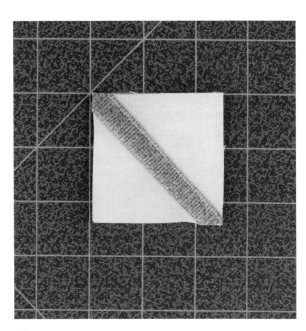

5   Finished stem block.

6   Lay out the 9 elements of the leaf block as shown. Sew rows together first.

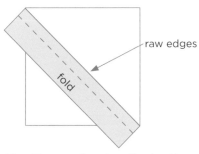

raw edges

fold

4A with raw edges together lay the folded rectangle along the center diagonal; stitch a ¼″ seam.

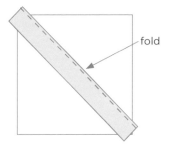

fold

4B press the folded edge over the stitching and topstitch the stem into place

4C trim

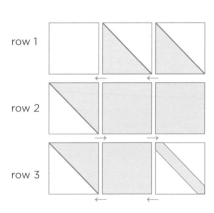

row 1

row 2

row 3

5 lay out all 9 elements of the leaf block as shown; sew rows first

3 make HSTs

For each block make 4 HSTs. Iron a crease diagonally across 4 solid squares. Pair each with a print square RST and sew on the crease. Trim ¼″ to one side of the stitching, press to the dark side. Return these to their group.

4 make the stem

Fold the 3½″ x 1½″ rectangle in half WST, press. Lay the raw edges diagonally across the center of a solid square. You can iron a fold into the square as a guideline if you wish. Stitch ¼″ along the raw edges of the folded rectangle. **4A**

Press the folded edge over the stitching line encasing the raw edges and top-stitch down. **4B** Trim to the square's shape. **4C** Repeat for each block.

5 build the block

Lay the 9 elements of the leaf block into 3 rows of 3. Watch the HST orientation! Sew the rows together first. Press seams in rows 1 & 3 in the same direction; row 2 in the opposite direction. Then sew the 3 rows together, nesting seams as you go. Repeat for all the groups.

Block size: 6½″ x 6½″
Yield: 72 blocks

6 arrange and sew

Lay the blocks into an eye-pleasing 8 x 9 setting. Just as before with the blocks,

build the rows first, then sew rows together. Press seams in odd rows to one side; in even rows to the other side. Press.

Quilt Center Size: 48½″ x 54½″

7 borders

From the inner border fabric cut (6) 1½″ strips. Follow steps in *construction basics* to attach to the quilt. **A-D** Press to the borders.

Cut (7) 4″ strips of outer border fabric. Attach to the quilt in the same manner as the inner border.

8 quilt & bind

Layer quilt top on batting and backing and quilt the way you like. Square up all raw edges.

Cut (7) 2½″ strips from binding fabric to finish. See *construction basics* for greater detail.

A

C  D

B

7 attach borders in sequence **A-D**;
  first inner border then outer border

Wacky Web quilt

quilt designed by NATALIE EARNHEART

I wish you could see my house at Halloween. I tend to go a little overboard with the decorating, dressing up, and partying. We don't do scary, we do fun. Either way, you wouldn't dare to come to one of my Halloween parties without a costume!

One year, when a few of my kids were teenagers, a couple of them decided they were too cool for costumes. Didn't I know that Halloween was kid stuff? They broke the news to us that they would be spending Halloween "hanging out" in the basement with their friends who were probably way cooler than me, their lame mom, who insisted on dressing up, covering the house in cheesy cobwebs and referring to green Kool-Aid as "witch's brew."

Halloween arrived and the self-assured teenagers descended to their downstairs lair. Upstairs we partied, playing games and eating spiderweb cupcakes and orange frosted treats. Everyone's costumes were so fun and I was busy considering who would win our prize for Best Costume.

Then the kids below experienced what came to be known as the Great Mouse Scare of '97. I didn't know what was going on, but I could hear a herd of teenage feet pounding up the basement steps. Well, I thought they had just decided to come up for snacks, which I warned them they wouldn't be getting without costumes. So I did what any loving mother who had been abandoned by her own children would do. I locked the door. I heard their muffled screams of protest and yelled back, "Not without costumes!" After a panicked minute or two my son yelled back, "Ok, we've got costumes, now LET US IN!"

I opened the door and in flooded a gaggle of shell-shocked teen-agers with the necks of their shirts pulled up over their heads...

Headless Horsemen! I guess the saying is true—necessity is the mother of invention!

As you might imagine, the commotion was caused by a mouse that I was assured was "bigger than our cat!!" We enjoyed the retelling of their story, while they enjoyed some snacks, and I got the entire family together for my Halloween Party. Win-win! If I had known a little mouse was all it would take, I'd have sent one down there myself!

Kids may outgrow Halloween (at least until they get old enough to enjoy it again!) but this Wacky Web Quilt is a fun, scrappy pattern for a beautiful quilt that you'll never outgrow.

materials

makes a 68" X 80" layer cake quilt

QUILT TOP

- 2 layer cakes, 2 different colorways
- 3 charm packs solid
- 1 yd border

BINDING

- ½ yd coordinating fabric

BACKING

- 4¾ yds **OR** 2 yds 90"

ADDITIONAL TOOLS

- Wacky Web template large
- Paper Piecing Triangles from MSQC
- Glue stick

SAMPLE QUILT

- **Artisan Spirit Shimmer** 42 by Northcott
- **Artisan Spirit Shimmer** 84 by Northcott
- **Bella Solids White** (98) by Moda Fabrics

1 cut

Cut all layer cakes into (4) 2½" strips each. Organize into light, medium & dark stacks each of blue and purple.

Use the large Wacky Web template to cut shapes from all but 6 of the solid charm squares.

2 paper piecing

Apply 1 strip of glue down the center of the triangle paper. Lay the solid cut shape in place. **2A**

One leg of the triangle will be striped in purples, the other blues. Place a dark layer cake strip RST along one side of the web shape. Stitch ¼" along the raw edges. **2B** Press open. **2C**

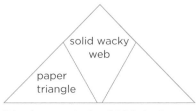

2A placement of solid fabric shape

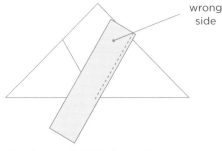

2B place strip RST along edge of solid fabric shape; sew ¼" seam

1 Cut the Wacky Web shape from the solid charm squares.

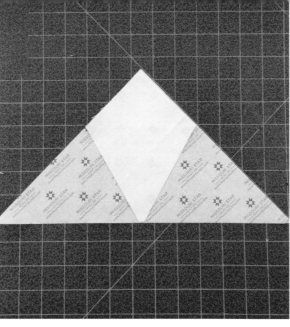

2 Run the glue stick down the center once. Then place the solid shape on the triangle paper as shown.

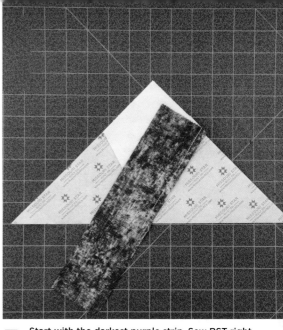

3 Start with the darkest purple strip. Sew RST right through the paper to one side of the Wacky Web shape with a ¼" seam.

4 Work from dark to light. Use blue strips on the other leg.

5 Turn upside down and trim the fabric to the paper triangle.

6 Remove the paper from the block. Because it has been perforated by the sewing needle, it will tear easily along seam lines.

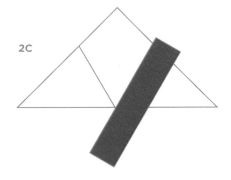

2C

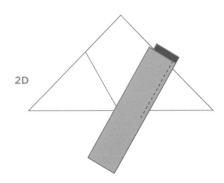

2D

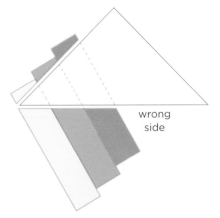

wrong
side

3A flip the triangle upside down;
trim excess fabric.

3B

4 turn all the solid wedges to the
center; sew into halves (see +
signs); then sew center seam

Add a second & 3rd strip—medium & light.
2D Repeat for the second leg but choose
the other colorway.

3 trim

Flip the triangle. With a ruler and rotary
cutter trim off excess fabric using the
paper as a trim guide. **3A** (*Diagram shows
only one side of the triangle complete.*)
Remove paper from the back. Press. **3B**

Many of the remaining strips can be used
again for other triangles. Return these

strips to the dark, medium & light stacks
to be reused. Make 120 triangles.

4 build block

Use 4 triangles per block. Turn the solid
wedges toward the center. Sew 2 pairs
of adjacent triangles together; press
seams in the opposite directions; then
sew both halves together nesting the
seams. Repeat 30 times.

Block size: 12½″ x 12½″
Yield: 30 blocks

5 arrange & sew

Lay the blocks out into a 5 x 6 setting.
Once you are pleased with the layout,
begin sewing blocks together side-by-
side to make rows. Press the seams in
odd rows to one side; to the opposite
side in even rows. Sew rows together
nesting seams as you go.

Quilt Center Size: 60½″ x 72½″

6 border

From the outer border fabric cut (8)
4″ strips. Follow steps in *construction
basics* to attach to the quilt. **A-D** Press to
the borders.

7 quilt & bind

Layer quilt top on batting and backing
and quilt the way you like. Square up all
raw edges.

Cut (8) 2½″ strips from binding fabric to
finish. See *construction basics* for details.

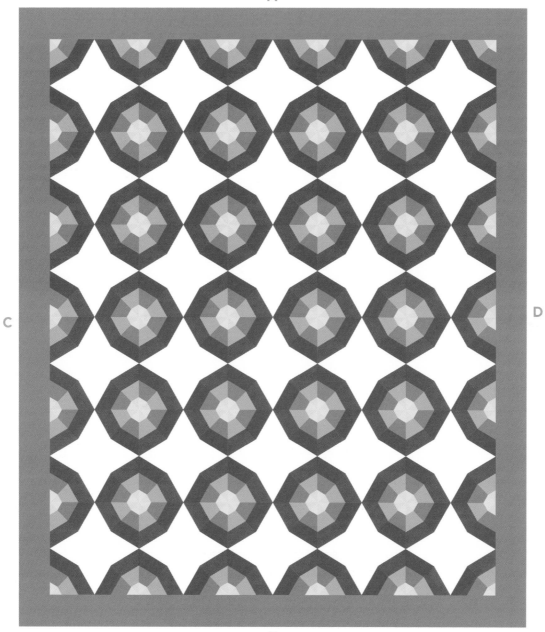

A

B

C

D

Jump Rings Quilt

quilt designed by NATALIE EARNHEART

I love to garden, but for a long time I didn't have enough space to grow everything I would have wanted. When we moved to Missouri, I suddenly found myself with a large yard and all the gardening space I could wish for. I went nuts! I planted tomatoes, peppers, beans, corn, pumpkins, squash, and zucchini. Plus the yard already had a few fruit trees. I was in gardening heaven.

Then came time to harvest. Most evenings I didn't cook dinner; I just walked out into the yard and picked us a meal. We ate BLTs, salads, fajitas, green beans, and corn on the cob until we thought we'd pop. Do you have any idea how many different baked treats can involve zucchini? I actually lost count.

Then we canned. Holy heirloom tomatoes did we can! That year, I filled so many jars I could have told you exactly how many green beans fit into a pint. When I closed my eyes at night to sleep, all I could see were vegetable peelings!

But eventually, I ran into a bigger problem. As earnestly as we tried, we just couldn't eat, freeze, or can all the food coming from our garden. I gave away baskets of peaches and piles of zucchini, but I just couldn't stay on top of it all. We ended up letting many of our peaches and apples drop and a few of the zucchini and tomatoes went back into the garden as compost.

Since that first year I've gotten a good handle on how much I can plant and preserve, so harvest is a very satisfying time of year for me. But there's still a sense of urgency to make use of the harvest before it's gone.

This is why the permanence of quilting is so appealing to me. When you make a quilt with quality fabric, it can last forever and become a treasured family heirloom. And heck, even if your kids don't like it and give it to Goodwill, someone will stumble on it and they won't believe their luck! The love and work that you put into your quilting doesn't disappear like a fall harvest—it will be used and loved year after year, harvest after harvest.

THERE'S NOTHING BETTER THAN A SUNNY AFTERNOON with your best friends and a lovely quilt!

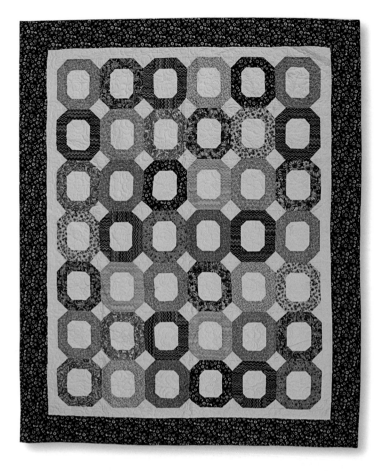

" The love and work that you put into your quilting doesn't disappear like a fall harvest—it will be used and loved year after year, harvest after harvest. "

materials

makes a 67" X 82½" layer cake quilt

QUILT TOP
• 1 layer cake
• 2¼ yds background fabric
• 1¼ yds border fabric

BINDING
• ½ yd coordinating fabric

BACKING
• 2¼ yds

SAMPLE QUILT
• **Indian Summer** by Benartex
• **Bella Solids Snow (11)** by Moda Fabrics

1 cut

Cut a layer cake into the following sections:

(2) 2½" x 10" rectangles

(2) 2½" x 5" rectangles

(4) 1½" squares

Repeat for a total of 42 layer cakes.

From the background fabric, cut:

(6) 5" WOF strips;

subcut into (42) 6" rectangles

(11) 2½" WOF strips;

subcut into (168) 2½" squares

(16 squares per strip)

The key to constructing this ring block is keeping all the pieces of one layer cake together.

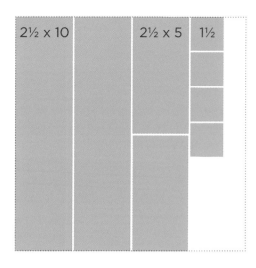

1 cut each layer cake

2 snowball center

Snowball the ring's center giving it the illusion of rounded corners. First iron a diagonal crease into the (4) 1½″ print squares. Lay each square RST on the corners of the 5″ x 6″ solid rectangle. Sew on the crease across the small squares. Complete all 4 corners using the same print. Trim seam allowance to ¼″ and press back. Keep this inner ring with the remaining cuts of the same layer cake. Make 42.

3 create the ring

Using the same print fabric as the snowballed corners, attach (2) 5″ print rectangles to the top and bottom of the block. Press to the print. Add the (2) 10″ strips to either side.

4 second snowball

Use the background 2½″ squares to snowball the block's 4 corners again following the same process in step 2. Trim. Press.

Block size: 9″ x 10″

5 arrange & sew

Arrange the blocks into a 6 x 7 eye-pleasing setting. Sew blocks together across in rows. Press seams to one side in even rows; to the opposite side in odd rows.

Sew rows together nesting seams as you go. Press.

Quilt Center Size: 51½″ x 67″

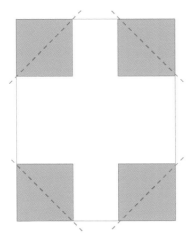

2 snowball the corners one block at a time

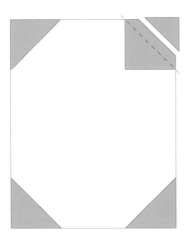

2 trim excess fabric; press

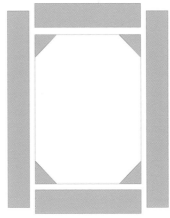

3 add top & bottom rectangles; then both sides

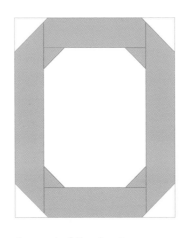

4 snowball the 4 outer corners with the 2½″ background squares

1 Snowball the solid center block with (4) 1½" squares of the same print.

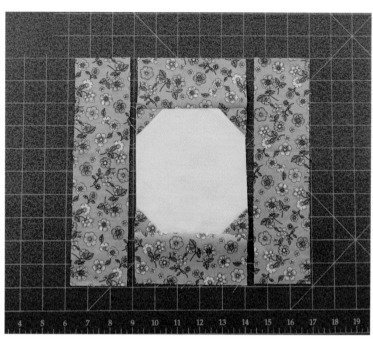

2 Add the top & bottom 5" strips first, then the 10" strips to the sides.

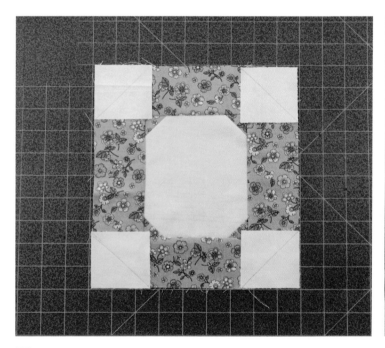

3 Snowball the block again but with 4 solid 2½" squares.

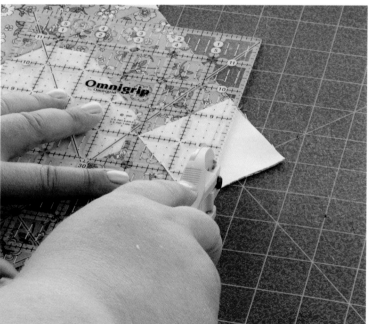

4 Trim to ¼" seam allowance.

6 borders

From the background fabric cut (7) 2½"
strips. Follow steps in *construction basics*
to attach to the quilt. **A-D** Press to the
borders.

Cut (7) 6" strips of outer border fabric.
Attach to the quilt in the same manner as
the inner border.

7 quilt & bind

Layer quilt top on batting and backing and
quilt the way you like. Square up all raw
edges.

Cut (8) 2½" strips from binding fabric to
finish. See *construction basics* for greater
detail.

REMEMBER, people will see your
quilts long after you're gone...not
your housework!

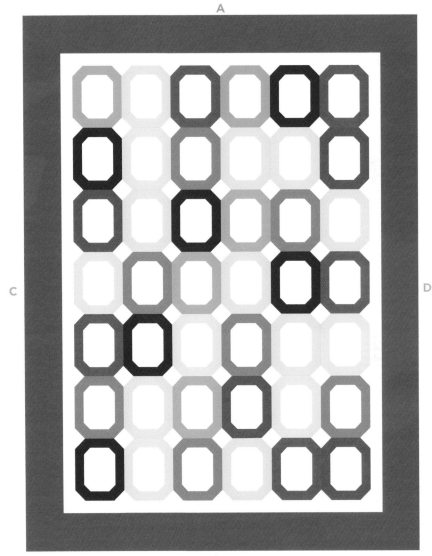

5 arrange in a 6 x 7 setting
6 attach inner & outer borders

Chopped
Block

quilt designed by JENNY DOAN

There were hundreds of times when the kids were little that I wished time would pass more quickly. I couldn't wait for the baby to sleep through the night, for the toddler to outgrow tantrums (ha!), for the kids to be old enough to stay home without a sitter, or for the teenagers to be able to drive themselves around.

But there were also moments, about a hundred a day, when I wished time would freeze and never move again: watching my three-year-old eat a banana with his fat little cheeks and perfect pink mouth; the time I caught a little one making up songs about fairies when she thought no one was around; when the girls had a foot race in the rain and didn't care that they ended up covered in mud; every time we cuddled in a heap to watch a movie or read a story and I didn't know whose foot that was or who was sitting on my arm. I took mental snapshots of these moments, willing them to stay forever, while knowing they couldn't.

> " . . . there were also moments, about a hundred a day, when I wished time would freeze and never move again . . . "

I've been accused of being sentimental, and I guess my personal stash of nostalgia-wrapped items is proof that I'm guilty. I have an odd-shaped piece of orange upholstery fabric that I inherited from my favorite great-aunt. Also in my possession is a box of scraps my mother cut from her bridesmaids' dresses. What will I ever use this fabric for? Probably nothing, but I just can't get rid of it. There are some things, like my collection of frozen memories, that I am just too attached to, things that I'm afraid to lose.

Sometimes this extends to new fabric, too. I make so many quilts that, for the most part, I've outgrown the hesitation I used to feel when I cut into beautiful fabric. But there are still those rare pieces—fabric too pretty or unique to cut, fabric that I fear I may never find the like of again—they are difficult for me to alter.

This quilt is just right for those pieces that you can't bring yourself to cut. If the print is big or the picture just won't be the same in small pieces, use it in this quilt and show it off. I guess there are some things in life that you can keep the same forever.

Now if only this trick worked for preserving moments.

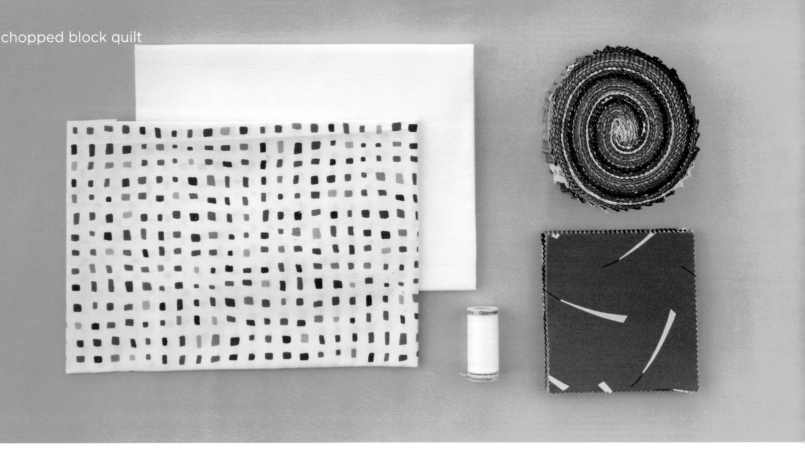

materials

makes a 82" X 93" jelly roll & charm pack quilt

QUILT TOP
- 1 print jelly roll
- 1 print charm pack
- 1 jelly roll + 1 yds background solid
- 1½ yd outer border

BINDING
- ¾ yd coordinating fabric

BACKING
- 7½ yds **OR** 3 yds 90"

SAMPLE QUILT
- **Daily Zen** by Michele D'amore for Bernartex
- **Bella Solids White (98)** by Moda Fabrics

1 cut block centers

From the print charm squares, select 21 and trim down to 4½."

From the background fabric cut:
    (3) 4½" WOF strips; subcut into (21)
    4½" squares

Yield: (21) solid 4½" squares
       (21) print 4½" squares

2 cut strip sets

Stay organized. Keep strips of the same print together in sets.

Begin with the print JR.
Make (21) **Set A** and (21) **Set B**.
Each **Set A** consists of (4) strips:

1 trim 21 print charm squares to 4½"; make (21) 4½" solid squares

Set A (2) 4½" (2) 8½"

Set B (2) 12½" (2) 8½"

2 make (21) Set A & (21) Set B in print JR; repeat for solid JR

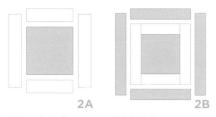

2A print charm + solid Set A
2B add print Set B=print center block

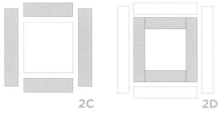

2C solid square + print Set A
2D add solid Set B=solid center block

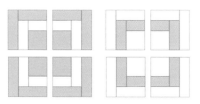

3A cut each block into fourths; keep them organized as pairs and piled in print center or solid center stacks

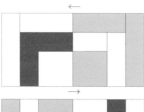

3B select 1 print center pair + 1 solid center pair to make a block

From *each* of 21 JR strips cut:
(2) 4½" rectangles
(2) 8½" rectangles
Each **Set B** is (4) strips:
From *each* of 21 JR strips cut:
(2) 8½" rectangles
(2) 12½" rectangles

Repeat with solid JR strips. Make (21) **Set A** & (21) **Set B** from the solid JR.

3 build blocks

If you consistently press to the print fabric, nesting seams will be easy as you sew.

Make print center blocks. Begin with a 4½" print charm square and a solid Set A. **2A** Attach:
(2) 4½" strips to top & bottom;
(2) 8½" strips to each side.
Next use a print **Set B**. **2B**
(2) 8½" strips to top & bottom;
(2) 12½" strips to each side.

Repeat for a total of (21) print center blocks. Repeat to make (21) solid center blocks: solid center + print **Set A** + solid **Set B. 2C-D**

Block size: 12½" x 12½"
Yield: (42) total blocks

4 cut & shuffle

Cut each block into fourths. **3A** Work at the corner of your cutting table. Leave the block in place and move around the corner of the table to make the next cut.

There will be 2 pairs from each block. Organize the pairs into (2) stacks: print center & solid center.

Select 1 pair from each stack. **3B** Arrange as shown. Sew blocks together to make a row (follow pressing arrows); then sew rows together. Nest all seams. Press.

Block size: 11½" x 11½"
Yield: (42) blocks

5 quilt center

Following the diagram, arrange the blocks into an eye-pleasing 6 x 7 setting. Maintain the pattern of "print-next-to-solid" from block to block and from row to row.

Once the position of the blocks is determined, sew them together in rows. Nesting seams will give the quilt a final polished look.

Press the seams in even rows to one side; in odd rows to the opposite side. Sew rows together to make the quilt center.

Quilt center size: 66½" x 77½"

6 borders

From the inner border fabric cut (9) 2½" strips. Follow steps in *construction basics* to attach to the quilt. **A-D** Press to the borders.

Cut (9) 6" strips of outer border fabric. Attach to the quilt in the same manner as the inner border.

7 quilt & bind

Layer quilt top on batting and backing and quilt the way you like. Square up all raw edges.

Cut (10) 2½" strips from binding fabric to finish. See *construction basics* for greater detail.

1 Cut 21 print charm squares down to 4½."

2 Use a print Set A to surround a solid block.

3 Follow with a solid Set B.

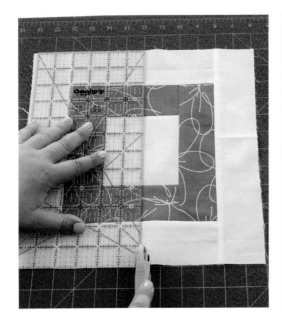

4 Cut the blocks in half twice.

5 Group the 4 sections into 2 pairs.

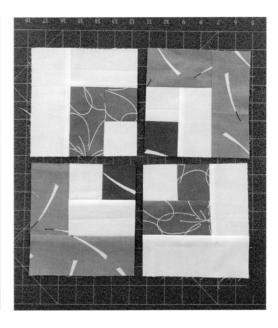

6 Use 1 pair of solid center blocks and 1 pair of print center blocks and arrange as shown.

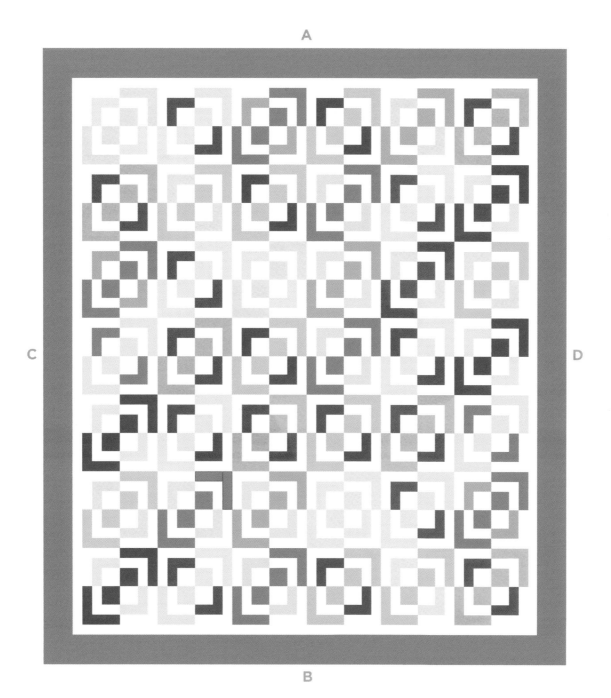

A

B

C

D

Happy
chicks
pincushion

designed by JENNY DOAN

When God created the earth, he must have spent an awful lot of time on the details. I mean, think about it. This planet would be perfectly capable of sustaining life with nothing more than a touch of sunshine, a little water, something to eat, and the right mixture of breathable air. Everything else is just bonus! Wildflowers of every color, vibrant sunsets, butterflies; white, sandy beaches, and sparkling white snow. Look around you! Whether the view out your kitchen window is a majestic mountain range or an endless sea of rolling, green fields, we are surrounded by beauty.

That remarkable beauty trickles all the way down to quilting. Growing up, my grandma made the most adorable petticoats and slips for all us little girls. She'd start with a pretty, silky fabric in soft pinks or blues and add fun

little touches of lace and rosebud details. Of course, no one else would ever see her handiwork, but she still wanted them to be beautiful, just because.

WHETHER YOU ARE THE GIVER OR RECEIVER, a cute pincushion is always a great gift! They can be collected, used and appreciated no matter how many you may already have!

Today, when I travel to teach quilting classes, some of my favorite things to see are all the unique pincushions. As I walk around the tables, I'll often stop to hold up a particularly cute pincushion so everyone can "oooh" and "ahhh." I love to see the creativity that goes into something as mundane as a holder for pins!

> " I think that human beings have an innate desire to make beautiful things that reflect God's own master stroke. "

We learned how to make this adorable chicken pincushion a couple of years ago at one of our guild meetings. It is such a charming little project to brighten up your sewing table. Of course, a pin-cushion doesn't have to be cute in order to do its job well, but it sure makes things a lot more fun!

I think that human beings have an innate desire to make beautiful things that reflect God's own master stroke. From music to painted masterpieces to intricate quilts, mankind has filled the world with amazing creations for thousands and thousands of years. Yes, we could survive with just the plain 'ole basics of life, but isn't it so much more wonderful to THRIVE surrounded by beauty?

materials

- 2 orphaned blocks the same size **OR** 5 charm squares ranging from light to dark.

- Contrasting scraps for chicken beak, tail and comb

- Stuffing, such as rice, soybeans, crushed walnut shells, lizard litter, or poly stuffing

OPTIONAL ITEMS
- Beads for eyes, yarn for comb, extra scraps for multiple tails or a lower beak

SAMPLE PIN CUSHION
- **Winter Enchantment** by Bee Sturgis for Quilting Treasures

Each log cabin block requires:

2  light (1¼, 2)

4  medium-light (2, 2¾)

5  medium (2¾, 3½)

3  medium-dark (3½, 4¼)

1  dark (1¼)

1A cut 2 rectangles for every size indicated in parentheses for (2) log cabin blocks

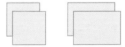

1B for example, from the light color strip, subcut into (2) 1¼″ squares & (2) 2″ squares

---

If you use 2 of your own orphaned blocks, skip to step 3.

1 log cabin blocks

Select (5) 5″ charm squares that range in value from light to dark.

From the darkest square cut (1) 1¼″ strip.

From the other 4 charm squares, cut (4) 1¼″ strips from each. Stack according to value: light, medium-light, medium, medium dark.

Subcut (2) rectangles of each size shown in parentheses in the list. **1A** & **1B** This will be enough for 2 log cabin blocks, or 1 chicken. There will be leftover strips.

2 sew the blocks

The 2 log cabin blocks are slightly varied. Make one at a time. The color value order that will be followed to construct the blocks is listed on the left in diagram **1A**. Begin with (1) dark square. Follow the sequence adding the shortest rectangle first from each color value. Each strip is placed at a 90° angle against the short end of the previous strip. Follow numbers & arrows moving <u>counterclockwise</u> around.

The second log cabin block is constructed as a *mirror image* of the first. Follow the color and size selection in the same number sequence as the first block, *but* change direction. Add strips <u>clockwise</u> this time.

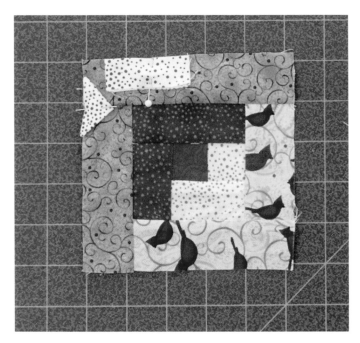

1 Choose a top corner. Place the beak and comb facing inside.

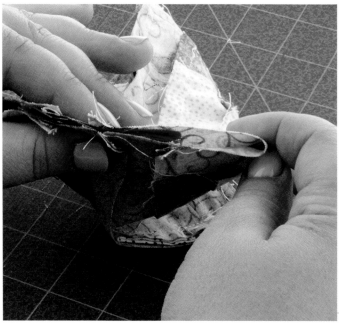

2 The last seam is pulled out and flattened. Notice the tail is centered between the top and bottom seams pointing inside.

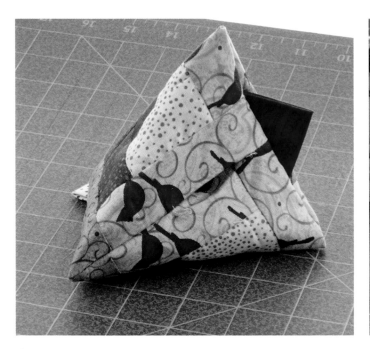

3 The opening is on the bottom ready to fill.

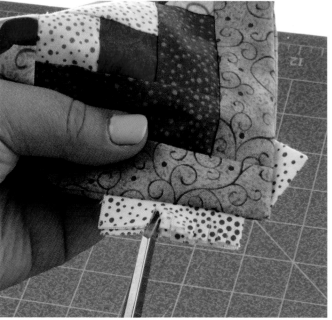

4 Clip the comb's raw edges and fluff.

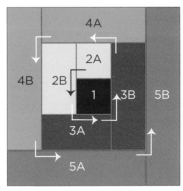

2 for each color value add the shortest rectangle first

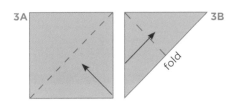

3 make prairie points from the 1½″ & 2½″ squares; press

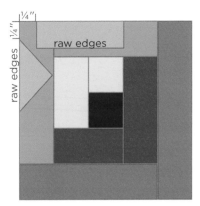

4 decide which is the top corner; set beak and comb on opposite sides ¼″ back from the corner

3 beaks & such

Make the following:

beak: 1½″ square

comb: 1¼″ x 2″ rectangle

tail: 2½″ square

Beak & Tail: Make prairie points from the squares. Fold each in half diagonally, then in half again. All raw edges will run along one side of the triangles and 2 sides will be finished folds. **3A-C** Press.

Comb: Fold the rectangle in half lengthwise and press.

4 sew

Decide which corner is the top. Place the prairie point beak ¼″ below on the lower side of the corner, folded edges facing in toward the block. Place the comb ¼″ from the corner along the top side. In this case, raw edges point toward the block. Place the second block RST on top matching orientations. Sew along those 2 sides.

5 bottom & tail

At the bottom edge sew the beginning of a seam and the end, leaving an opening in the middle. Backstitch on each side of the opening. **5A**

The last open edge of the block remains. Pinch the middle of this side, pulling the 2 blocks apart. Then flatten them, matching the top and bottom seams. **5B** Place the tail between the blocks pointing inside. Line up all raw edges. **5C** Pin.

Sew across from fold to fold.

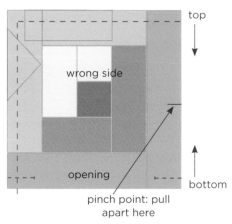

pinch point: pull apart here

5A leave an opening at the bottom; backstitch

5B on the last open side, pinch the middle and pull apart; flatten; match top and bottom seams

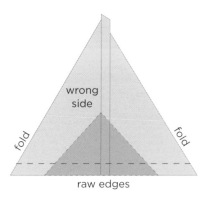

5C transparent top-down view of last seam to be sewn; tail centered between blocks; top seam showing; one block to the left of center; one to the right; sew across

6 finishing

Clip corners. Turn, push out the corners gently. Clip the chicken's raw-edge comb and fluff. Finger press the raw edges of the opening to the inside. Stuff the head portion with a little bit of poly fiber. Fill the remainder of the chicken with your choice of stuffing. Whipstitch opening closed.

Periwinkle
table topper

designed by JENNY DOAN

True friendship thrives not on big, momentous occasions, but on those simple gestures that stitch us together forever. When Carole moved in across the street, she quickly made it clear that we were going to be friends and there was nothing I could do to stop it. Some people are just born with a talent for friendship. They have the remarkable ability to make you feel comfortable, understood, and connected almost immediately. There's no need for empty pleasantries or impersonal politeness. They just insert themselves right into the nitty gritty of your life. Carole is such a person—the ultimate friend.

She's also slightly crazy, but only in the best ways! I'll never forget the time Carole stopped by unannounced on my birthday. She waltzed into my living room dressed up in her frilly pink prom dress from high school, crown on head and wand in hand. "The Birthday Fairy is here to wish you a happy day!" she sang as she leaped dramatically toward me with a quart of chocolate ice cream in her hand.

Then, she placed a sparkling, plastic tiara on my head and a "birthday queen" banner across my chest. And it only got

funnier from there! Carole dismantled a bouquet of helium filled balloons and carefully tied the string of each one to small sections of my shoulder-length hair. When she was finished, I had a dozen or so hunks of hair floating straight up from my head! We laughed ourselves silly as she pranced her way out the door as suddenly as she had arrived, singing in her best opera voice, "Haaappy Birthday to Youuuuuu!"

Of course, it isn't always crazy shenanigans with Carole. She is an excellent listener and always gives the best advice. She laughed with me as we weeded the flower garden together, and cried by my side as I mourned the loss of a loved one. Through it all, she never missed a chance to prove her friendship in countless little ways.

Carole is a master gift giver. I can't count the times she stopped by with a fun little present for any and every occasion. Now that we live miles apart, she is still sure to send a cute outfit or storybook every time a new grandbaby is born in our family.

I think the key to being a good friend is helping others to feel valued. A small gift now and then can say, "I'm thinking of you. I appreciate you. You are special to me." That's why I love this little "mug rug." It's quick to put together, but cute and personal. It would make the perfect gift for a teacher or neighbor. When we take the time to show our love to others through these little acts of kindness, great things can happen.

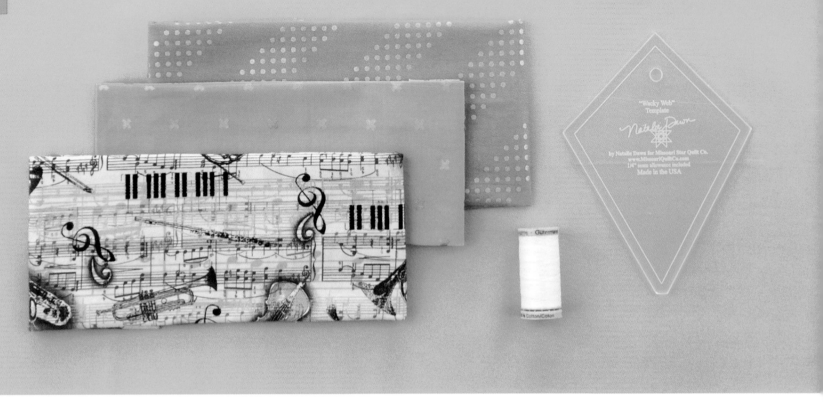

materials

makes a 12" X 12" table topper

- 6 charm squares
- 1 fat quarter **OR** a 12" scrap for backing
- large MSQC wacky web template
- 12" square of fusible fleece

SAMPLE TABLE TOPPER
- **Cotton + Steel** for RJR
- **All That Jazz** by Karen Foster for Robert Kaufmann

1 cut shapes

Select (6) 5" charm squares. They can be all the same, 2 each of 3 different fabrics or all different. You decide which look you are after!

Using the large Wacky Web template, cut the charm squares.

2 sew

Arrange the shapes with the tails all pointing to the center in the order you want them. Sew together in 2 groups of 3 along the sides that taper to a point. **2A** Sew the final center seam matching the points in the middle. **2B** Press.

1 cut Wacky Web shape from 6 charm squares

1 Cut 6 Wacky Web shapes from charm squares.

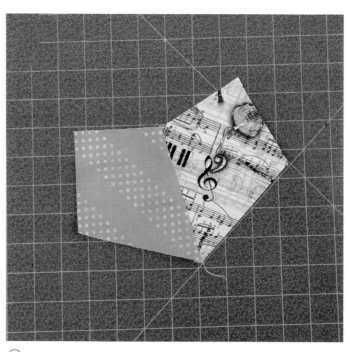

2 Sew the shapes together along the long sides.

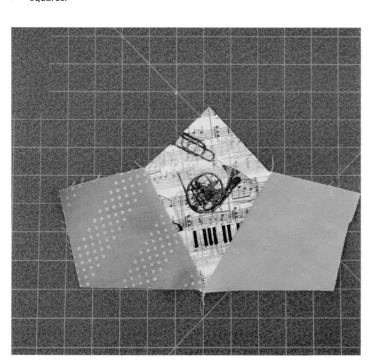

3 Make 2 sets of 3.

4 Cut the fusible fleece using the periwinkle top as a pattern.

3 fuse

Use the mug rug top as a pattern to cut out its shape from the fusible fleece. With the bumpy side to the back of the mug rug top, fuse the fleece into place.

4 add the back

Lay the top RST (right sides together) on the backing and rough cut around it. Sew with the fusible fleece showing on top. Make sure to leave a 3" opening. Begin and end by backstitching. The opening should start after passing an inside corner and end before a periwinkle point. See diagram 4.

5 finishing

Trim the back clipping the star points and the inside corners as you go to reduce any extra bulk. Turn inside out gently pushing the star points into shape. Turn the raw edges of the opening to the inside. Press.

Follow Jenny's continuous quilting suggestion and the opening will be topstitched closed as you quilt!

Begin at the point marked "start." Travel past the center to periwinkle #1 and stitch around. Always pass through the center except in periwinkle #3. Here follow along the outside edge crossing over the beginning stitches to get to #4. Continue quilting as before, finishing with the last side of periwinkle #4.

2A sew the long sides

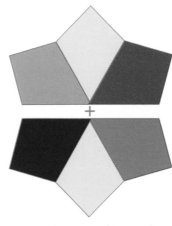

2B sew 2 groups of 3 together

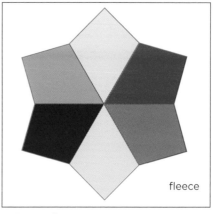

3 use the top as a pattern to cut the fusible fleece

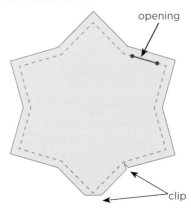

4 trim the backing; clip and turn

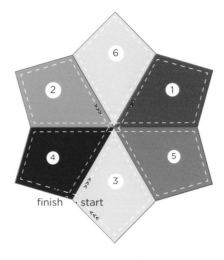

5 Jenny's continuous quilting

Self-binding
baby blanket

designed by JENNY DOAN

A quilt or receiving blanket is a classic gift for a new baby, and the Self-Binding Baby Quilt is a perfect option because not only it is adorable, but it comes together in a flash. I love to see a tiny, new babe wrapped up in a soft, warm quilt. But the sweetest thing is when that simple quilt becomes the newborn's special "blankie."

A few years ago, I made a baby quilt for a friend who was pregnant with her first son. By little Spencer's first birthday, that quilt had become his best friend and constant companion.

When he was just over a year old, Spencer's mom noticed that he favored one corner of his blankie. To everyone else, all four corners of the quilt were completely identical, but Spencer could always tell the difference, even in the dark! He gave a special name to his precious corner: "The Paka Loco." The Paka Loco had an almost magical ability to calm this wild boy, even on his naughtiest days. He would

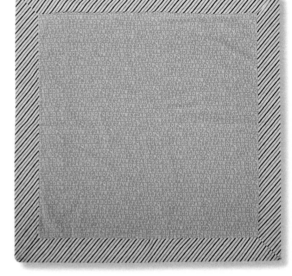

hold the corner up to his sweet little nose, close his eyes and take a deep, peaceful breath.

Spencer grew quickly, as little boys tend to do, and his interests turned to cars and trucks and balls and trains—anything fast and noisy. But wherever he went, he always made sure that his blankie was nearby. It was common for Spencer to take a quick break from his play to run over to the quilt, explaining with a twinkle in his eye, "I need to smell my Paka Loco."

Over the years that baby quilt traveled everywhere from

A BABY IS SUNSHINE AND MOONBEAMS
and more brightening your world as never before.
-author unknown

Grandma's house to the movie theater to the campground. It went through about a million cycles in the washing machine and was worn to a perfect, cozy softness. It functioned as a cape and a hiding place, but its most important role was that of comforter.

I love to give quilts to new babies and always hope that my quilt will become that one special blankie-the one that adds that extra bit of comfort and imagination to those magical first few years of life. This Self-Binding Baby Quilt is so sweet that although it only takes minutes to make, it's sure to provide days and days of cozy cuddles!

" . . . the sweetest thing is when that simple quilt becomes the newborn's special "blankie". . . "

materials

makes a 35" X 35" baby quilt

BLANKET
- 1¼ yds back
- 1 yd inside

SAMPLE BLANKET
- **Cozy Cotton** by Robert Kaufman for Robert Kaufman

1 cut

From yardage cut 2 large squares:

- (1) 40" for back
- (1) 30" center

2 pin

As strange as it may seem, this just may be the most important step!

Find the center of each side of the 2 squares and mark with a pin. Folding the side in half and finger-pressing is a quick and easy way to find and mark the centers.

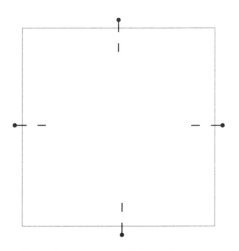

2 mark centers on all sides of both squares with pins

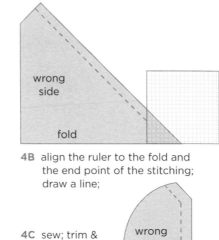

3 sew from the center out stopping ¼" before the edge of the smaller square; backstitch

4B align the ruler to the fold and the end point of the stitching; draw a line;

4C sew; trim & clip each corner

wrong side

wrong side

fold

wrong side

wrong side

fold

4A at a corner bring 2 adjacent sides of the smaller square together folding it in half to the inside

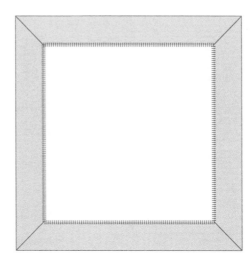

5 finish by stitching around the inside square closing the opening at the same time

3 sew

Lay the smaller inside square on top of the larger back square RST (right sides together). Start with one side. Line up the raw edges, pin the centers and continue pinning along the edge from the center out.

Starting at the center pin of one side, sew a ¼" seam stopping ¼" before the small square's edge. Backstitch at the end. Repeat 2 more times. For the last side, leave a 5" opening in the middle, backstitching on both sides of the opening.

4 miter corners

Work with 1 corner at a time. At one corner bring the 2 adjacent sides of the small square together folding it to the inside. **4A** The smaller square is now hidden inside the larger square. Lay the blanket on a flat surface. The wrong side of the large square will be folded along one side; a line of stitching will be visible along the opposite side. **4B** Place a ruler on the fold and draw a line from the end of the stitching to the fold. Sew on that line. Trim ¼." Clip. **4C** Repeat with the other 3 corners.

5 finishing

Turn the blanket inside out through the opening. Gently push out the corners. Turn the raw edges of the opening to the inside and press. Use a straight, zig-zag, blanket or decorative stitch to sew along the seam where the 2 squares meet. This will close the opening as well.

1 The seam is sewn from the center out. Note the 2 dots on the smaller square. Start at the center dot and stop ¼" before the end of the square, at the 2nd dot.

2 The smaller inside square will be stitched along all sides. At the corner bring the sides of the smaller square together, fold to the inside.

3 The outer square will fold as well—like a long tail stretching beyond the end of the inner square.

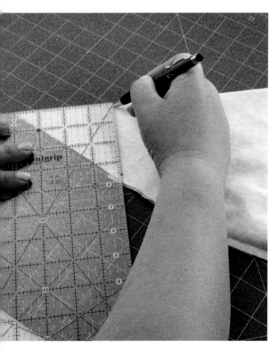

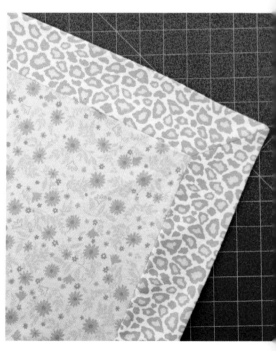

4 With one side of the ruler running along the fold, line up the other side of the ruler to the stitching's endpoint. Draw a stitching line.

5 After stitching on the line trim to ¼" seam allowance.

6 The corner will miter on its own when the blanket is turned inside out.

How to back a quilt

The fabric that makes up the back side of your quilt is called the backing. The backing needs to be larger than the quilt top. This allows for fabric that is taken up during the quilting and for stabilization when using a quilting frame. Always add 8″ to both the length and width measurements so you have an extra 4″ all around.

There is a wide variety of beautiful wide backings available that range in size from 60″-120″ wide with the most common width being 108.″ These can be used on many of your quilts. Selecting backing from wide goods is as easy as measuring your quilt top, adding 8″ and cutting your back fabric to this measurement.

Sometimes, though you will want to piece your backing, using regular quilters cotton, or scraps! Standard calculations assume 42″ of usable fabric can be cut from 44/45″-wide fabric. In order to back a quilt most economically, think in increments of 42, 84 & 126 (Figures A-C). Then ask yourself which side of your quilt (width or length) is closest to one of these numbers but does not exceed it. For example, a quilt top of 60 x 80 needs a backing that is 68 x 88. Become a quilting Goldilocks: 42″ is too little for either side, 126″ is too big, but 84″ is just right! The quilt's length (88) exceeds the 84″ limitation. But using the 84″ width to span the 68″ side will work. The seam will run vertically. Therefore use the 88″ side to

calculate yardage. Double it because you need 2 panels of fabric and voilà, you have your backing requirement. (See the Figure A) Fold the yardage in half lengthwise and sew at least ½″ to the inside of the selvage along one side. Cut the fold, remove the selvage and you're done.

In some cases, you may have a quilt top that is almost the same size as your backing. Turn this into an opportunity to get creative on the back. You could add your leftover blocks and fabric from the project or sew together several scraps to make a piece large enough. One method of expanding the back that we do NOT recommend is a

quilt backing that has a type of border all the way around it. These are difficult to quilt because of the way quilts are loaded onto modern quilting machines. Watching the back to monitor whether its borders remain straight is nearly impossible to do during the quilting process. This means the borders often end up being crooked or too close to the binding.

So here's a work-around that will spice up your quilt backs and add a dimension of creativity: you can cut the fabric lengthwise near the middle or some place that creates a pleasing proportion, maybe a 1:2 ratio. Insert a long strip in between these two pieces of fabric using a ½" seam allowance. Cutting the main fabric in the middle keeps the pieced seams on the back away from the final finished edge when the quilt is trimmed. Seams on the back that are near the edge of the finished quilt top can be visually awkward and add extra bulk to the binding if they are too close to the edge.

Backing your quilt today has evolved quite a bit from the muslin sheets we used to use. We always love to see the variety and beauty that goes into every quilt. Many times the backings are as beautiful as the tops! Have fun with it!

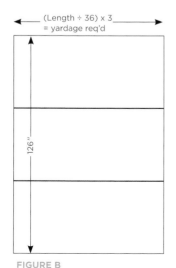

FIGURE A

42"

84"

(Length ÷ 36) x 2 = yardage req'd

Quilt top
60 X 80

BACKING FORMULA:
width + 8" x length + 8"
Example quilt top: 60 x 80
Backing needed: 68 x 88

The 84" dimension of figure A will cover the 68" width. Calculate yardage for the 88" side.

CALCULATION:
88÷36=2.44; 2.44 x 2 = 4.88 or 5 yds

(Length ÷ 36) x 3 = yardage req'd

126"

FIGURE B

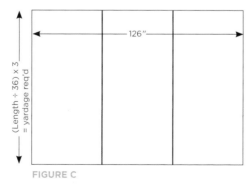

126"

(Length ÷ 36) x 3 = yardage req'd

FIGURE C

chopped block

QUILT SIZE
82" X 93"

DESIGNED BY
Jenny Doan

PIECED BY
Cassie Nixdorf

QUILTED BY
Jamey Stone

QUILT TOP
1 print jelly roll
1 print charm pack
1 jelly roll + 1 yd bkgnd solid
1½ yds outer border

BINDING
¾ yd coordinating fabric

BACKING
7½ yds **OR** 3 yds 90"

SAMPLE QUILT
Daily Zen by Michele D'amore
for Bernartex

Bella Solids White (98) by Moda
Fabrics

ONLINE TUTORIALS
msqc.co/choppedblock

QUILTING
Square Meander

QUILT PATTERN
pg 56

 TIP: *Want to make a different size? No problem, check out these and other patterns online!*

disappearing hourglass

QUILT SIZE
72¼" X 83½"

DESIGNED BY
Jenny Doan

PIECED BY
Stephen Nixdorf

QUILTED BY
Jamey Stone

QUILT TOP
1 print layer cake
1 solid layer cake **OR** 2½ yds solid
½ yd inner border
1¼ yds outer border

BINDING
½ yd coordinating fabric

BACKING
5 yds or 2¼ yds 90"

SAMPLE QUILT
Miss Kate by Bonnie &
Camille for Moda Fabrics

Bella Solids Snow (11)
by Moda Fabrics

ONLINE TUTORIALS
msqc.co/hourglass

QUILTING
Curly Twirly Flowers

QUILT PATTERN
pg 16

happy
chicks

DESIGNED BY
Jenny Doan

PIECED BY
Jenny Doan

PROJECT MATERIALS
2 orphaned blocks the same
size **OR** 5 charm squares ranging
from light to dark.

Contrasting scraps for chicken
beak, tail and comb

Stuffing, such as rice, soybeans,
crushed walnut shells, lizard
litter, or poly stuffing

OPTIONAL ITEMS
beads for eyes, yarn for comb,
extra scraps for multiple tails or
a lower beak

SAMPLE
Winter Enchantment by Bee
Sturgis for Quilting Treasures

ONLINE TUTORIALS
msqc.co/happychicks

PATTERN
pg 64

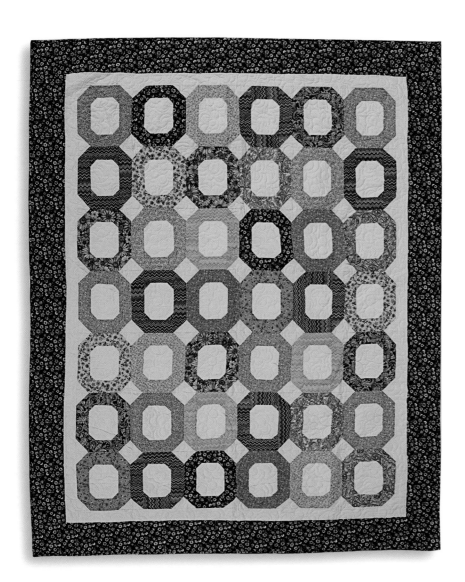

jump rings

QUILT SIZE
67" X 82½"

DESIGNED BY
Natalie Earnheart

PIECED BY
Natalie Earnheart

QUILTED BY
Amber Weeks

QUILT TOP
1 layer cake
2¼ yds background fabric
1¼ yds border fabric

BINDING
½ yd coordinating fabric

BACKING
2¼ yds

SAMPLE QUILT
Indian Summer by Benartex

Bella Solids Snow (11) by Moda
Fabrics

ONLINE TUTORIAL
msqc.co/jumprings

QUILTING
Daisy Days

QUILT PATTERN
pg 48

lovely
leaves

QUILT SIZE
58" X 64"

DESIGNED BY
Jenny Doan

PIECED BY
Natalie Earnheart

QUILTED BY
Sandi Gaunce

QUILT TOP
1 jelly roll print
2¼ yds solid
1 yd outer border

BINDING
½ yd coordinating fabric

BACKING
3¾ yds coordinating fabric

SAMPLE QUILT
Burlap Solids by Bernartex

Bella Solids White (98) by
Moda Fabrics

ONLINE TUTORIALS
msqc.co/lovelyleaves

QUILTING
Cotton Seed

QUILT PATTERN
pg 32

periwinkle
table topper

TABLE TOPPER SIZE
12" X 12"

DESIGNED BY
Jenny Doan

PIECED BY
Jenny Doan

PROJECT MATERIALS
6 charm squares
1 fat quarter **OR** a 12" scrap for backing
large MSQC wacky web template
12" square of fusible fleece

SAMPLE TOPPER
Cotton+Steel for RJR

All That Jazz by Karen Foster
for Robert Kaufmann

ONLINE TUTORIALS
msqc.co/periwinkletabletopper

TABLE TOPPER PATTERN
PG 72

self-binding baby blanket

BLANKET SIZE
35" X 35"

DESIGNED BY
Jenny Doan

PIECED BY
Stephen & Cassie Nixdorf

BLANKET
1¼ yds back
1 yd inside

SAMPLE BLANKET
Cozy Cotton by Robert
Kaufman for Robert Kaufman

ONLINE TUTORIALS
msqc.co/selfbindingbaby

PATTERN
PG 80

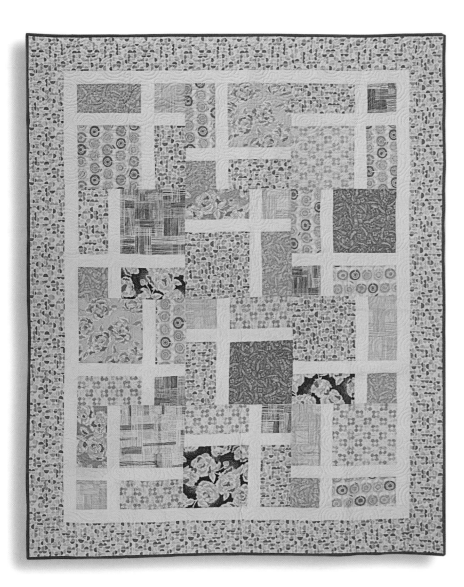

slice of life

QUILT SIZE
64" X 80"

DESIGNED BY
Jenny Doan

PIECED BY
Jenny Doan

QUILTED BY
Cassie Martin

QUILT TOP
1 print layer cake
½ jelly roll **OR** 1½ yds solid fabric
1¼ yds outer border

BINDING
½ yd coordinating fabric

BACKING
5 yds 44" wide **OR** 2 yds 90" wide

SAMPLE QUILT
Palermo by Erin Mcmorris for Westminster

Bella Solids White (98) by Moda Fabrics

ONLINE TUTORIALS
msqc.co/sliceoflife

QUILTING
Sticky Buns

QUILT PATTERN
PG 8

 TIP: *Want to make a different size? No problem, check out these and other patterns online!*

tag
team

QUILT SIZE
50" X 55½"

DESIGNED BY
Natalie Earnheart

PIECED BY
Jenny Doan

QUILTED BY
Betty Bates

QUILT TOP
½ print charm pack
2 solid charm pack
½ yd inner border
¾ yd outer border

BINDING
½ yd coordinating fabric

BACKING
3¼ yds

SAMPLE QUILT
Elementary by Sweetwater
for Moda Fabrics

Bella Solids Snow (11)
by Moda Fabrics

ONLINE TUTORIALS
msqc.co/tagteam

QUILTING
Arc Doodle

QUILT PATTERN
PG 24

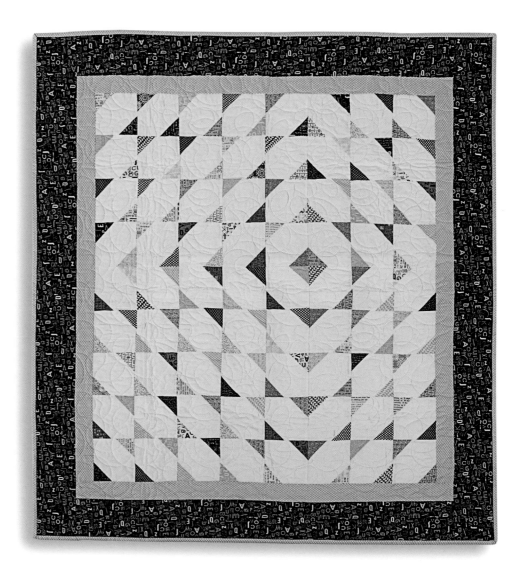

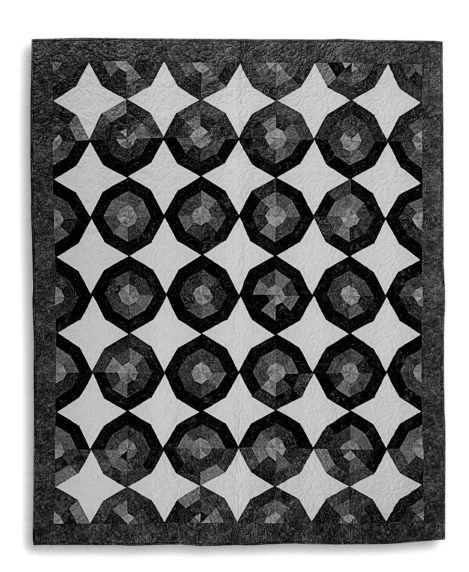

wacky web

QUILT SIZE
68" X 80"

DESIGNED BY
Natalie Earnheart

PIECED BY
Natalie Earnheart

QUILTED BY
Megan Gilliam

QUILT TOP
2 layer cakes, 2 different colorways
3 charm packs solid
1 yd border

BINDING
½ yd coordinating fabric

BACKING
4¾ yds **OR** 2 yds 90"

ADDITIONAL TOOLS
Wacky Web template large
Paper Piecing Triangles from MSQC
Glue Stick

SAMPLE QUILT
Artisan Spirit Shimmer (42)
by Northcott

Artisan Spirit Shimmer (84)
by Northcott

Bella Solids White (98)
by Moda fabrics

ONLINE TUTORIALS
msqc.co/wackyweb

QUILTING
Arc Doodle

QUILT PATTERN
PG 40

general guidelines

- All seams are ¼" inch unless directions specify differently.

- Cutting instructions are given at the point when cutting is required.

- Precuts are not prewashed; therefore do not prewash other fabrics in the project

- All strips are cut WOF

- Remove all selvages

- All yardages based on 42" WOF

ACRONYMS USED

MSQC	Missouri Star Quilt Co.
RST	right sides together
WST	wrong sides together
HST	half square triangle
WOF	width of fabric
LOF	length of fabric

pre-cut glossary

CHARM PACK
- 1 = (42) 5" squares or ¾ yd of fabric
- 1 = baby
- 2 = crib
- 3 = lap
- 4 = twin

JELLY ROLL
- 1 = (42) 2½" strips cut the width of fabric or 2¾ yds of fabric
- 1 = a twin
- 2 = queen

LAYER CAKE
- 1 = (42) 10" squares of fabric: 2¾ yds total
- 1 = a twin
- 2 = queen

The terms charm pack, jelly roll, and layer cake are trademarked names that belong to Moda. Other companies use different terminology, but the sizes remain the same.

When we mention a precut, we are basing the pattern on a 40-42 count pack. Not all precuts have the same count, so be sure to check the count on your precut to make sure you have enough pieces to complete your project.

press seams

- Use a steam iron on the cotton setting.

- Iron the seam just as it was sewn RST. This "sets" the seam.

- With dark fabric on top, lift the dark fabric and press back.

- The seam allowance is pressed to the dark side. Some patterns may direct otherwise for certain situations.

- Follow pressing arrows in the diagrams when indicated.

- Press toward borders. Pieced borders may demand otherwise.

- Press diagonal seams open on binding to reduce bulk.

binding

- Use 2½" strips for binding.

- Sew strips end-to-end into one long strip with diagonal seams, aka plus sign method (next). Press seams open.

- Fold in half lengthwise WST and press.

- The entire length should equal the outside dimension of the quilt plus 15" - 20."

plus sign method

Diagonal seams are used when straight seams would add too much bulk.

- Lay one strip across the other as if to make a plus sign RST.

- Sew from top inside to bottom outside corners crossing the intersections of fabric as you sew. Trim excess to ¼" seam allowance.

- Press seam open.

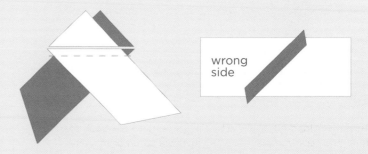

wrong side

attach binding

- Match raw edges of folded binding to the quilt top edge.
- Leave a 10" tail at the beginning.
- Use a ¼" seam allowance.
- Start in the middle of a long straight side.

miter binding corners

- Stop sewing ¼" before the corner.
- Move the quilt out from under the pressure foot.
- Clip the threads.
- Flip the binding up at a 90° angle to the edge just sewn.
- Fold the binding down along the next side to be sewn.
- Align the fold to the edge of the quilt that was *just sewn*;
- Align raw edges to the side *to be sewn*.
- Begin sewing on the fold.

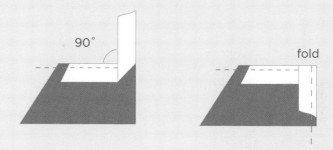

close binding

MSQC recommends **The Binding Tool** *from TQM Products to finish binding perfectly every time.*

- Stop sewing when you have 12" left to reach the start.
- Where the binding tails come together trim excess leaving only 2½" of overlap.
- It helps to pin or clip the quilt together at the two points where the binding starts and stops. This takes the pressure off of the binding tails while you work.
- Use the plus sign method to sew the two binding ends together, except this time when making the plus sign, match the edges. Using a pencil mark your sewing line since you won't be able to see where the corners intersect. Sew across.
- Trim off excess; press seam open.
- Fold in half WST and align all raw edges to the quilt top.
- Sew this last binding section to the quilt. Press.
- Turn the folded edge of the binding around to the back of the quilt and tack into place with an invisible stitch or machine stitch if you wish.

borders

- Always measure the quilt center 3 times before cutting borders.
- Start with the width and measure the top edge, middle and bottom.
- Folding the quilt in half is a quick way to find the middle.
- Take the average of those 3 measurements.
- Cut 2 border strips to that size.
- Attach one to the top; one to the bottom of the quilt.
- Position the border fabric on top as you sew. The feed dogs can act like rufflers. Having the border on top will prevent waviness and keep the quilt straight.
- Repeat this process for the side borders, measuring the length 3 times.
- Include the newly attached top and bottom borders in your measurements.
- Press to the borders.

PATCHWORK MURDER

PART 3

Charmed

——— *A JENNY DOAN MYSTERY* ———

written by Steve Westover

MK rubbed the tears and exhaustion from her eyes while she and Jenny sat in the hallway waiting for the police. A slick-haired, stylishly attired hotel security director arrived first with an entourage of hotel staff including the dayshift manager.

"I'm Brubeck," he said before asking some cursory questions. To avoid saying anything that could implicate her in wrongdoing MK remained silent while Jenny answered his questions. After a quick peek inside the room, Brubeck exited and then barked orders to a staff that appeared shell shocked that such an unsavory crime could take place in The Harrington. "Would you please come with me," Brubeck asked Jenny and MK as he stepped in the direction of the elevators.

"We'll wait right here, thank you," Jenny replied.

"It wasn't a request," Brubeck said.

Jenny reached to her side until she found MK's hand. She squeezed. "Unless you forcefully remove us, we're happy to wait right here for the police."

Brubeck studied the women with droopy eyes and then leaned a shoulder against the wall. "Then we'll wait together." Ten minutes felt like an hour before the first uniformed police officers arrived to secure the scene. Before long the hallway became a circus of confusion and credentials. Medical examiners, forensic investigators, and hotel guests all added to the commotion.

Homicide Detective Harry Scanlan joined the fray wearing a black straight-off-the-rack Sears special and a hideous lime green and hunter orange paisley necktie that reeked of the seventies. It hung cockeyed and loose. Scanlan looked like he'd rolled straight out of bed, suit and all. Kind of like me, Jenny thought. His strawberry blond hair looked like it had been clipped with sheep shearers but was too short to diminish his handsome features. Jenny glanced at his bare ring finger. He appeared too young to have already given up on his appearance, especially for an unmarried man, but he wore his sloppiness with a boyish charm.

"Scanlan," Brubeck greeted through clenched teeth.

"Brubeck," Scanlan acknowledged with a low growl. He glanced at Jenny and MK, raised his chin slightly and then walked into the hotel room.

Jenny leaned toward the doorway to look inside. Brubeck attempted to block her view so she stepped around him to watch Scanlan kneel beside the body, lift the duvet and then drop it.

"Ma'am, would you mind stepping back?" Brubeck said.

Jenny glanced at a uniformed officer who didn't seem bothered by her interest. "I would actually," she replied as she continued watching Scanlan. He spoke briefly to a woman wearing a black windbreaker with "Medical Examiner" blocked on the back. She listened closely but only picked out one word. "Stabbed." It was enough. Scanlan then spoke with the lead forensic investigator before he returned to the hallway.

Detective Scanlan's gaze rested briefly on Brubeck but then refocused on Jenny and MK. He rubbed his hand roughly over his mess of a haircut. "Good morning, ladies. Got a little bit of a problem here, don't we? Which one of you found the body?"

He spoke with enough of a lilting Midwest drawl that he reminded Jenny of home. She explained, cautiously at first, how she had come upon the corpse and how she had met Bruno the night before. But then she felt herself relax and the words flowed. Jenny had nothing to hide.

"And what about you," Scanlan asked turning his attention to MK. "Why were you in the room?"

Jenny had been dying to ask the same question but with so many people around had urged MK to remain silent to avoid self incrimination. Before MK could answer Detective Scanlan's question Jenny spoke up. "Is MK a suspect? Does she need an attorney?"

Scanlan exuded charm as he turned to MK. "You tell me. Did you do anything wrong?"

MK shook her head vigorously. "No."

"Then there's nothing to worry about, is there?" Scanlan said. "I'm just trying to get a feel for what happened. If you'd be more comfortable in an interrogation room I can arrange that."

Jenny bristled. "Detective, surely that's not necessary," she said.

He seemed to consider the option for a moment and then shook his head. "No. Not necessary. As long as you're one hundred percent truthful with me."

Brubeck scoffed. "Very official, Scanlan."

Scanlan smiled at the man. "You can leave now."

Brubeck's jaw clenched but then he skulked away.

"I'll let you know when I need you," Scanlan said loud enough for Brubeck to hear over the din of activity. "I know where to find you."

"You two friends?" Jenny asked.

Scanlan's lips parted as if preparing to answer but then he turned. "MK, please tell me why you were in the room."

MK cleared her throat and squeezed Jenny's hand. "Same reason as Jenny, really. When Bruno didn't deliver our bags I went looking for him. He wasn't in the lobby and the front desk acted like he didn't exist."

"OK, so what brought you to this room?" Scanlan queried.

"There was a man on the shuttle with us last night. I remembered him because I thought he was a little unusual."

"Unusual? How?" Scanlan asked.

"A man riding a shuttle for a quilting conference is odd. How many men do you know who quilt?" MK asked.

"You'd be surprised," Jenny said. "A lot of men quilt. I saw this shotgun themed quilt once and..." Scanlan cleared his throat and Jenny stopped in the middle of her story. "Sorry."

MK shrugged and then shared a nervous glance with Detective Scanlan. She continued. "He was a little guy and I recognized him when he got on the elevator with me. I wanted to ask if he received his luggage but he gave off this creepy vibe."

"Did you ask him?" Jenny asked anxiously. She looked down at her feet. "Sorry."

"No," MK said. "I was nervous. He got off first but when the door was closing I decided I'd better ask so I got off too. He was already around the corner. He's fast for a short guy. By the time I turned the corner he was already at his door half way down the hall."

"You followed a 'creepy vibe' man to his hotel room door?" Jenny asked, her head shaking. "Sorry... again." Scanlan smirked. "What happened next?"

"His door opened."

"You mean he opened his door?" Scanlan corrected.

"No. His door opened. Bruno stuck his head out and looked up and down the hallway. I was probably twenty yards away but he didn't seem to recognize me. The little man squeezed through and the door shut."

"So you found Bruno and you knew he had your luggage. What did you do?" Scanlan asked.

MK licked her lips and gulped nervously. "I didn't do anything."

"You got into the room somehow," Scanlan pressed. "You must have done something."

"I'm getting to it." MK stopped for a moment as she sniffed the air. Farther down the hallway hotel staff pushed a cart and then knocked on a door. "Do I smell bacon?"

"Focus," Scanlan chided.

MK's stomach grumbled audibly. "I didn't know what to do so I just stood there. Then the door opened again. The same little guy hurried out of the room in my direction so I pretended to fumble for my room key. He looked mad. After he turned the corner I hurried to the room. I may not know the creepy guy but I kind of knew Bruno so I thought I could trust him. I mean, he worked for the hotel. Why shouldn't I?"

"So you approached the door?"

"Yes. I knocked and Bruno opened. His eyes bugged out."

"He was surprised to see you?" Scanlan asked.

"Yeah, he was surprised. He grabbed my wrist and pulled me inside." MK held up her wrist and grabbed it to model what Bruno had done. "I was freaking out. I didn't know what was going to happen. I started to hyperventilate. He tried to calm me down. He told me to leave and not come back."

Jenny's attention hung on every word. "Then what?" she asked nervously.

"Well, first, I noticed the luggage rack loaded with our bags. He could tell I was suspicious. He grabbed the back of my arm and yelled at me. It was actually more of a whisper but it felt like a yell. He told me to leave. He was about to push me out the door when there was a soft knock. Bruno got all panicky. He shoved me into the bathroom and told me to stay quiet. He told me not to come out for anything. He told me to trust him. Before I could say anything I was standing in the dark with the bathroom door closed. My heart was pounding so hard."

Jenny looked protectively at her niece. "Oh honey. I'm so sorry."

"It's my fault. I was stupid."

Detective Scanlan made notes in a pocket sized notebook. Jenny wanted him to say something comforting to MK like "No, it's not your fault," or "You didn't do anything wrong." But he didn't. MK still needed to convince him.

MK continued. "So I stood there with my ear to the door trying to listen. They talked and laughed. Then they were quiet for a long time and I didn't know what was going on. I was in there forever. It was late and I was getting seriously tired. I didn't know what to do. I mean, what if the little guy had to use the bathroom? He'd see me. Bruno acted scared of him so I figured I should be too. I sat in the tub and closed the curtain to hide."

"And...?"

MK thought for a moment. "Nothing. That's it. After my heart stopped pounding and I could breathe normally again I must have dozed off."

"What time did all of this happen?" Scanlan asked.

"Sometime after midnight. I'm not sure, really. My phone was dead. I couldn't even call Jenny." MK watched Detective Scanlan's face for any sign of sympathy or understanding. "I woke up when I heard Jenny. You know the rest."

"Detective, you can see she's exhausted. Let me take her back to our room to get some rest; maybe some breakfast. You know how to find us," Jenny said.

Scanlan considered the women and then rubbed the back of his neck. His crooked lips turned up. "You've been very helpful. Just don't go anywhere." He handed MK his business card. "Call me if you think of anything else." He looked at her long, but not like a detective staring down a suspect. "Call me," he repeated. The boyish charm was back.

After a quick stop in the dining room for a bagel and some bacon Jenny eased MK into bed. "Stay here and rest," Jenny said. I'll be back in a while."

MK bolted up into sitting position. Even in the darkness Jenny could see the uneasiness in her eyes. "Where are you going?" MK asked.

"Don't worry sweetie. I just realized our bags are still in Bruno's room. I'm going to see if we can get our things." Jenny & MK sat for a moment in silence. "Scanlan's pretty cute, don't you think?"

MK groaned like an embarrassed teenager as she lay on her side, her back to Jenny. "You're not setting me up with Detective Scanlan. He wants to put me in jail.

"Nah. He's flirting."

"Don't even think about it."

"Who, me?" Jenny rubbed MK's back and pulled the covers to her shoulders. "I wouldn't dream of intruding in your love life."

"Uh huh...right."

Jenny stood and as she closed the double doors she asked, "Would you like me to call your mom to let her know what happened?"

MK nodded. "Thank you." She closed her eyes. "You won't be long, will you?"

"I'll be back soon. Don't you worry about a thing," Jenny soothed. "I'll take care of everything. The worst is over."